The Owl and the Nightingale

by the same author

poetry
ZOOM!
XANADU
KID
BOOK OF MATCHES
THE DEAD SEA POEMS
MOON COUNTRY (with Glyn Maxwell)
CLOUDCUCKOOLAND
KILLING TIME
SELECTED POEMS
TRAVELLING SONGS
THE UNIVERSAL HOME DOCTOR
TYRANNOSAURUS REX VERSUS THE CORDUROY KID
OUT OF THE BLUE
SEEING STARS
PAPER AEROPLANE (Selected Poems 1989–2014)
STILL
THE UNACCOMPANIED
SANDETTIE LIGHT VESSEL AUTOMATIC
MAGNETIC FIELD

drama
ECLIPSE
MISTER HERACLES (after Euripides)
JERUSALEM
HOMER'S ODYSSEY
THE LAST DAYS OF TROY
THE ODYSSEY: MISSING PRESUMED DEAD

prose
ALL POINTS NORTH
LITTLE GREEN MAN
THE WHITE STUFF
GIG
WALKING HOME
WALKING AWAY
A VERTICAL ART

translation
SIR GAWAIN AND THE GREEN KNIGHT
THE DEATH OF KING ARTHUR
PEARL

SIMON ARMITAGE

The Owl and the Nightingale

With Illustrations by
CLIVE HICKS-JENKINS

faber

First published in 2021
by Faber & Faber Limited
Bloomsbury House, 74–77 Great Russell Street
London WC1B 3DA

Typeset by Donald Sommerville
Printed in Latvia by Livonia Print

A CIP record for this book
is available from the British Library

ISBN 978–0–571–35729–1

4 6 8 10 9 7 5 3

MIX
Paper from
responsible sources
FSC
www.fsc.org
FSC® C002795

CONTENTS

INTRODUCTION

A narrator describes entering a remote valley in summer, where an owl and a nightingale are engaged in a bitter disagreement. It is a quarrel that continues for the better part of eighteen hundred lines of verse, in a style or genre sometimes described as 'comic debate poetry', and although the poetry is indeed comic and even hilarious on occasions, the word 'debate' lends a tone of intellectual politeness to what is at times a medieval slanging match. The fact that the birds are conversing in the language of humans is never explained or excused, and our unwitting acceptance of this situation from beginning to end can be taken as a confirmation of poetic achievement.

Of the many mysterious poems to have survived from the Middle Ages, *The Owl and the Nightingale* is one of the most mysterious of all. Despite expert investigation and analysis from many different angles, its date of composition is still a matter of speculation, with almost a hundred years separating the earlier and later possibilities. At lines 1091 and 1092 of the manuscript the nightingale invokes the name of 'King Henri', adding, 'Jesus his soule do merci'. The reference implies the king is dead, but is this Henry II who died in 1189, or Henry III, who wore the crown for fifty-six years until passing away in 1279? Two other monarchs occupied the throne during that period; the idea that the poem can't be confidently assigned to a particular reign, let alone a year or even a decade, seems to darken its shadowy beginnings. 'A twelfth- or thirteenth-century poem' is often how *The Owl and the Nightingale* is described.

Dating the poem's original composition would be easier if we knew who wrote it, but we don't. One candidate is a Master Nicholas of Guildford, a resident of Portesham in Dorset apparently, who is mentioned on two occasions in the poem as a man of sound judgement, someone who might objectively settle the dispute between the warring birds. Indeed the flawlessness of his character is one of the few things the birds are able to agree on. However, if it seems to make sense that a named person within the poem is likely to be its author, it seems just as likely to me that the author could be deflecting attention away from his own identity, or even sending up a third party with sycophantic praise. In this translation I have replaced Master Nicholas with the name of a poet who has a more reliable connection with the text. Further to the subject of authorship, I have referred to the narrator and the poet as 'he' in this introduction, but only through a sense of informed speculation based on the literary norms and precedents of the era. And interestingly, both the owl and the nightingale of the poem are female.

If authorship were established this might help throw light on the geographical origins of the poem (and vice versa), but on this topic, too, there is no consensus of opinion. The analysis of vocabulary, dialect words and regional spellings in Middle English poems often helps to pinpoint, or at least narrow down, their place of composition. In the case of *The Owl and the Nightingale*, locations as far apart as Kent and the West Midlands have been proposed, as well as Wessex – an area that would include most of Britain's southern coast and parts of the southwest.

Uncertainty in regard to all those issues both reflects and reinforces hesitancy about the poem's ultimate meaning. Clearly the birds, with their personalities, habits, abilities and physical characteristics, are representatives of particular ways of life and philosophical outlooks. This is especially true in relation to their Christian faith, and many critical commentaries focus on the extent to which the birds draw on biblical teaching to provide their themes and support their arguments. However, their individual claims to a religious and moral high ground are often undermined by contradictions in logic and descents into decidedly un-Christian rancour. The fact that their dispute remains unresolved at the end of the poem (despite the intervention of a wren, and with several other species of bird turning up to lend muscle or opinion) only adds to the ambiguity surrounding the author's intentions. That said, poetry of historical eras is always of more interest when it seems relevant and relatable to the contemporary reader, and on this front *The Owl and the Nightingale* does not disappoint. The dialogue between the birds resonates with issues that preoccupy latter-day society, including matters of identity, culture, the right to be heard and class distinctions. The superior tones of the nightingale clash and contrast with the more pragmatic attitudes of the owl, the song of one trying to win out over the screech of the other. Questions of personal hygiene, toilet habits, parenting skills, dietary preferences and sexual conduct also enter their bickering, alongside more elevated disagreements on the themes of individuality, survival, community and conscience, all traded in uncompromising, adversarial terms. If the poem was designed as an allegorical pastiche of humanity's predilection for vitriolic disagreement, then the two birds would not be out of place several centuries later, wrestling for 'control of the narrative' in an internet chat-room or across social media platforms.

But if the poem's overall significance remains elusive, what is not in doubt is the quality of the writing or, more specifically, its poetics. To produce a work of nearly nine hundred rhyming couplets written in near-regular metre (iambic tetrameter) requires stamina and patience. It also insists on an exceptional level of creative ingenuity if the poem is to stay agile and alert from beginning to end. There is great inventiveness on display here, and the kind of authorial self-awareness and subtlety that distinguishes literature from mere information, and transforms the studied documentation of an idea into something we call art.

There are two surviving manuscripts, one held by the British Library (MS Cotton Caligula A.ix (C), ff. 233ra–246ra) and one held by Jesus College, Oxford (MS 29 (J), ff. 156ra–168vb), both thought to have been copied from a single original or 'exemplar', now lost. Nuanced differences between the two versions are a matter of great importance and excitement to scholars of the poem; they are of less concern in this translation, though for the most part I have followed the British Library version.

I have described my working processes and my reasons for taking on these old anonymous poems, and my interest in medieval poetry generally, in introductions to other translations and in published lectures. But experience tells me that for the everyday reader, perhaps picking this book off the bookshelf out of idle curiosity (and thank you, if you have), one question comes to the fore. How can English be translated into English? I hope that question can be answered relatively quickly by quoting the first four lines of the original poem, which read as follows:

> Ich was in one summer dale
> In one suþe diȝele hale
> Iherde ich holde grete tale
> An hule and one niȝtingale

Middle English can be very crudely characterised as a form of English spoken and written in Britain from the arrival of William the Conqueror to the first printed editions of Chaucer's *Canterbury Tales*. The Middle English alphabet included the two letters thorn (þ – similar in this instance to 'th') and yogh (ȝ – similar in this instance to 'gh'), now obsolete. Knowing how to pronounce those letters allows a twenty-first-century reader to give voice to passages in the poem and develop a reasonable sense of what is being said. But line two is tricky because it contains words we no longer use and whose definitions are somewhat blurred, even to experts. The word hale (corner? place? location? hollow? glade?) isn't going to earn its keep in a contemporary rendition, so immediately a new rhyming couplet is called for, which will inevitably require changes to preceding words. Medieval sentence structure presents as archaic to modern ears, so a certain amount of grammatical reshaping is also necessary. And some words, even if they have retained their inherent meaning over several hundred years, have acquired new and sometimes unhelpful connotations, just as some modern words might feel anachronistic or out of place, no matter how accurate their definitions. Add to this the need to position words at particular locations in a line to conform to the prescribed rhythm of the poem, and something of the nature and scale of the task can be imagined.

It is interesting to speculate that seven or eight hundred years ago, all the uncertainties surrounding the poem as I have described them were probably not uncertainties at all, but very obvious facts. Except, that is, for the skill and verve of the author, who seems to have produced a work of unprecedented craft and virtuosic style in excess of the literary achievements of the period. Whatever audiences it reached, as readers or listeners they must have been mightily impressed by the poem's theoretical enquiries and commanding use of language, and greatly entertained by its two main characters, whose verbal sniping and sparring has the authenticity of actual speech. If the poem is erudite and articulate, it is also idiomatic and at times vulgar, drawing on everyday experiences, deploying colloquial registers, and appealing to our common understanding of human behaviour, albeit ventriloquised through the voices of two birds. The poem is almost a play, with an owl and a nightingale vying for the spotlight, and ultimately it is the theatrical and dramatic qualities of their monologues I have attempted to capture and replicate in this translation.

Simon Armitage

THE OWL AND THE NIGHTINGALE

One summer's day I overheard
a mighty war of words disturb
a peaceful & secluded dale;
between an Owl & Nightingale
barbed comments flew, now soft, now loud,   5
but always heartfelt, wounding, proud.
The birds, both swollen up with anger,
hurled abuse at one another,
taking turns to slate & curse
what in the other bird was worst,   10
with insults being especially strong
when rubbishing the other's song.

The Nightingale took up proceedings
from the corner of a clearing,
perching on a handsome bough   15
with blossoms hanging down & round,
beside a densely knotted hedge
entwined with reeds & bright green sedge.
She gloried in that branch; it formed
a kind of stage, & she performed   20
the music of her repertoire
as if she played a pipe or harp,
as if each bright, melodious note
were not the product of a throat.

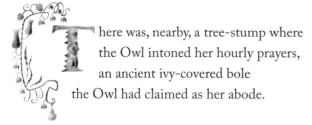

There was, nearby, a tree-stump where   25
the Owl intoned her hourly prayers,
an ancient ivy-covered bole
the Owl had claimed as her abode.

The Nightingale clapped eyes on her
& shot the Owl a filthy glare,   30
disgusted by that horrid creature's
loathsome, nauseating features.
'Freak, why don't you disappear?
It sickens me to see you here.
Your ugly presence guarantees   35
to throw my fluting out of key.
In fact whenever you turn up
my jaw locks & my heart won't pump.
As for your tuneless yodelling
it makes me want to spit, not sing.'   40

he Owl was silent until dusk,
        by which time she was on the cusp
        of rage, her lungs about to burst
    through holding back her angry words,
    her heart about to pop. She yowled,   45
        'How does my music strike you now?
You tell yourself that I can't sing
but I'm not one for twittering.
You ridicule me & you mock,
snipe from the cover of the copse,   50
but if you flew that branch of yours
I'd make you welcome in my claws
(bring on that day before too long!)
& then you'd sing a different song!'

    t which the Nightingale remarked,   55
        'As long as I'm alert & sharp
        in open ground or on the wing
    your menace has a hollow ring.
    As long as I keep to the hedge
        your words are simply worthless threats.   60
I've seen the ruthless way you rip
those birds who can't escape your grip,
& how you like to sink your pincers
into little larks & finches.
That's why feathered creatures hate you,   65

drive you from their patch, berate you
with their screams & cries, & why
they rise & mob you when you fly,

        & why the tiniest of tits
        would gladly tear you bit from bit.   70
        You really are a gruesome sight
        in ways too many to describe:
        your neck's too thin, your trunk's too small,
        your head is bigger than . . . your all!
        Your coal-black eyes are weirdly broad   75
& look like they've been daubed with woad,
& glare as if you'd like to feast
on anyone within your reach.
Your bill is sharp & bent & hard –
a flesh-hook with a buckled barb –   80
that issues – loud & all day long –
some caterwaul you call a song.
You threaten me, & say your feet
will catch & mulch me into meat;
a frog, though, underneath the mill-wheel,   85
surely makes a truer Owl meal?
Snail & mouse & squelchy slug
are more your right & proper grub.
You roost by day & fly by night
which proves that something isn't right.   90
You are repellent & impure,
you & those filthy chicks of yours,
that brood of dirty-looking pests
you're raising in a filthy nest.
They soil the den they're living in   95

[6]

until their droppings reach their chins
then stand about as if they're blind,
which brings this truism to mind:
"Accursed be the wretched beast
that makes its toilet where it feeds."   100
One year a falcon left her brood
& in her absence from the wood
you slipped into the clutch to lay
your ugly-looking egg one day,
& after several weeks had passed   105
& several of her chicks had hatched
she brought her young ones meat to eat
but noticed as the fledglings ate
that one half of the nest was neat,
the other in a squalid state.   110
The bird was livid with her young,
who felt the rough edge of her tongue.
"Explain who made this shameful mess.
No child of mine would foul the nest.
You're victims of a sneaky trick,   115
so tell me who committed it."
The chicks, first one & then another,
all sang out, "It was our brother,
him whose head sits like a boulder,
shame it's still perched on his shoulders.   120
Fling his foulness to the deck
& where he lands he'll break his neck."
The falcon's chicks would not tell fibs;
she plucked the stray bird from their midst
& threw it to the forest floor   125

[7]

where crows & magpies gouged & tore.
This fable, though it isn't proof,
delivers an essential truth:
expect no good of any trace
from him born to a lowly race.   130
He might mix with a better class
but can't escape his commonness,
& even in a decent nest
a rotten egg's a rotten egg.
An apple might roll far & wide   135
& leave its family tree behind,
but at its core it still betrays
its starting place & early days.'

Then after hectoring so long
the Nightingale broke out in song,   140
her tune as vibrant & as sharp
as music streaming from a harp.
The Owl took in the songbird's sound,
her eyes fixed firmly on the ground,
& sat there ready to explode,   145
like someone choking on a toad.
She knew full well the other bird
was baiting her with wounding words,
but answered her, 'Why don't you show
yourself out here & then we'll know   150

who wears the fairer face, & who
is finest feathered – me or you.'
'No thanks, your talons bite like nails.
I'd rather not become impaled
on sets of claws so hard & strong   155
they grip their prey like iron tongs.
You mean to snare me with untruth;
that's Owl behaviour through & through,
& I'll be paying your advice
no heed because it's laced with lies.   160
Admit the shame of who you are,
your crooked traits are now laid bare
& so are those deceits you cloak
when spending time with decent folk.
And if you deal in dirty business   165
check it's done without a witness;
treachery becomes disgrace
when played out in a public place.
Though knowing how to duck & weave
protects me from your evil schemes;   170
you thrash about, all boast & brawn,
but I do better with my brain
than you with all your thuggish strength,
& on this branch – its breadth & length –
I have my castle. "He who flies   175
shall win the flight." So say the wise.
Enough, though, of this bickering,
such barneys are belittling.
Let's start afresh, & this time act
with greater courtesy & tact.   180

We don't see eye to eye, that's plain,
but both would make a stronger claim
without hostility or spite.
Let's state with dignity & pride
our points, positions & beliefs   185
in measured tones & reasoned speech.'

The Owl replied, 'A magistrate
is needed to adjudicate.'
    'That's easy,' said the rossignol,
'his name stands ready on my tongue.   190
The person who should arbitrate
is Master Simon Armitage.
He's skilled with words & worldly wise
& frowns on every form of vice.
In terms of tunes, his ear can tell   195
who makes a din & who sings well.
He thrives at telling wrong from right
& knows the darkness from the light.'

he Owl considered what she'd heard,
then after pondering declared,
'Agreed, he'll tell the honest truth,
though he was reckless in his youth
& spooned a Nightingale or two
& other passerines like you.
And yet he has cooled down a lot
& doesn't lust for you of late
& wouldn't, through some lingering love,
set me below & you above.
His sense of justice won't be harmed
by your submissions to his heart.
Mature & of a balanced mind,
all indiscretions left behind,
ignoring every vulgar cause
he steers a straight & proper course.'

chooled in the art of rhetoric
the Nightingale's response was quick.
'So tell me, Owl, why is it true
you do as evil creatures do?
The one nocturnal dirge you sing
is woeful & self-pitying
& those unlucky souls who hear
are terror-struck with morbid fear.
The squawks you aim towards your mate

200

205

210

215

220

disturb the ears they penetrate.
Both dolt & genius have found
your singing makes a weeping sound.
You sleep by day & fly by night,
which worries me, & well it might;
all things preferring wrong to right
adore the dark & hate the light,
& every sinful creature needs
the night-time to obscure its deeds.
A proverb, vulgar but of note
(a phrase King Alfred said & wrote),
repeated frequently: "He slinks
away who knows his own bad stink."
That summarises perfectly
your fly-by-night activities.
And something else occurs to me:
in total blackness you can see
but once the dawn dispels the dark
you struggle telling branch from bark!
And of those beings who by day
are sightless, this is what they say:
they're ne'er-do-wells & vagabonds
whose shady dealings know no bounds,
whose sneaky schemes & escapades
no decent person can escape,
they tread a shadowed path & shun
the lanes & ways lit by the sun,
& you're the very same, the type
who lives her life avoiding light.'

225

230

235

240

245

250

She listened for what felt an age,
the Owl, then flew into a rage.
'You're called a Nightingale,' she spat,   255
'but blabbermouth's more accurate.
Your monologues are all-consuming,
rest your tongue & stop assuming
that you've won the day & own
the argument. Give me my turn   260
& keep your trap shut while I speak
& listen closely while I seek
a rational & sincere revenge
without recourse to verbiage.
You say by day I hibernate,   265
a fact I won't repudiate,
but hear me while I clarify
the wherefore & the reasons why.
My beak is powerful & strong,
my claws are sharp & very long,   270
& rightfully I share these traits
with others of the owlish trade.
No man can criticise my pride
in feeling kinship with my tribe.
Look at my features & you'll find   275
ferocity personified,
so all the tiny birds abhor me,
flitting through the understorey,
slighting me with squeaks & squawks
& flying at me in their flocks   280
when all I want to do is rest
in peaceful silence on my nest.

[15]

I'll fare no better if I shriek
& curse my enemies, or speak
the kind of oaths & foul abuse 285
& filthy talk that shepherds use.
Instead of wasting words with knaves
I'd rather look the other way.
The wise have noted more than once
that he who argues with a dunce 290
might just as well compare his jaw
against an oven's yawning door.
And now a saying comes to mind,
a proverb that King Alfred coined:
"Be careful not to waste your life 295
where strife & quarrelling are rife;
keep well away from fractious fools."
A wise Owl, I obey those rules.
A further point that Alfred makes
is quoted far & wide. It states: 300
"Those mixing with a filthy kind
shall never leave the dirt behind."
Therefore a hawk is none the worse
if crows along the marsh rehearse
their jeers & jibes, then swoop & squawk 305
as if they mean to fell the hawk.
The hawk, though, follows sound advice:
he lets them shriek, then off he flies.
And there's a further charge you bring,
the accusation I can't sing, 310
& that my song is one long moan,
a painful, monotonal drone.

It isn't so. My voice, being true,
emits a rich, melodious tune.
You twitter, so for you a song   315
that doesn't cheep & chirp is wrong.
My call is deep & bold & proud
& booms out with a horn-like sound,
while yours pipes like a tinny reed
sliced from a thin unripened weed.   320
My song is best, yours pleases least,
you witter like an Irish priest!
I sing at dusk – the proper hour –
& then at bedtime sing once more,
then sing again when midnight chimes;   325
my songs are governed by those times.
I see the distant dawn draw near
& watch the morning star appear
then from my throat a note is shaped
that summons workers to their trade.   330

But you sing all & every night
from sunset through to morning light,
the whole night long you sing a song
that prattles on & on & on,
an exhibitionist display   335
that chirps away throughout the day
& causes trauma in the ears
of anybody living near,
a song so cheap it has no worth
for people anywhere on earth.   340
For as a rule, a thing that pleases
rankles if it never ceases;

[17]

harps & pipes & songs of birds
eventually disturb the nerves,
just as the cheeriest of scores   345
seems not so cheery any more
if endlessly performed. Your song
is likewise wastefully prolonged.
A noble stance that Alfred took
(it's written down in many books):   350
"When overdone, true virtue fades.
With overkill, real value wanes.
Indulgence, surplus & excess
do not equate to more, but less,
& what goes on relentlessly   355
infuriates eventually."
The only everlasting good
is found within the realm of God:
its basket constantly provides
yet stays replenished to all sides.   360
God's wondrous empire knows no end,
forever giving, never spent.

A further slander: you have dared
to say my vision is impaired,
assuming that I fly by night   365
because I'm blinded by the light.
But clearly you are telling lies;
I know that I have perfect eyes
since there's no dim or darkened state
my piercing gaze can't penetrate.   370
I have defective sight, you say,
because I never fly by day,
but skulking through those hours, the hare
is master of the watchful stare.
Flushed from his form by hunting hounds   375
at breakneck pace away he bounds
down steep & curved & narrow tracks,
all twists & turns & clever tricks,
until with leaps & darts he speeds
towards the cover of the trees.   380
Coordination of that kind
is not accomplished by the blind!
I hide away by day but share
outstanding eyesight with the hare.
When fearless soldiers march to war,   385
advancing on all fronts, the corps
engaging evil foreign powers
& fighting through the darkest hours,
I keep them company, my flight
a flag above them in the night.'   390

eft to her thoughts, the Nightingale
then mulled things over for a while,
not confident she could deny
the soundness of the Owl's reply,
because with that robust defence   395
the Owl had spoken truth & sense.
Perhaps her judgement had been wrong
to let the rumpus last this long,
& now it was her turn to speak
her logic might sound false or weak.   400
But she was bold & held her nerve,
&, wisely, spoke with guts & verve,
& looked her foe straight in the face.
The timid voice will lose the case;
a rival prospers if he sees   405
you run – stand firm though & he flees,
or met by fortitude he'll flip
from fierce wild boar to gelded pig.
And so, despite all doubts & fears,
the Nightingale was loud & clear.   410

She answered, 'Owl, why do you croon
a miserable & gloomy tune
each winter? Like a hen in snow
complaining of its grief & woe
you gripe & groan all season long,   415
then come the summer you play dumb!
Pure malice means that you can't bear
the happiness that others share,
& your resentments fume & burn
wherever pleasure takes its turn.   420
You're like some old curmudgeon, riled
by every laugh or blissful smile,
a true-born killjoy fuelled by spite
who hates a sweet or cheerful sight.
You smirk & simper when you hear   425
of men whose faces stream with tears.
When wool gets tangled up with hair
the weaver weeps & you don't care.
That's where you stand – on sorrow's side –

so when the snow lies deep & wide   430
with every bird & beast forlorn,
you drone your dirge from dusk to dawn.
But gladness spreads when I arrive
to every animal alive;
folk eagerly anticipate   435
my coming, which they celebrate!
Then flowers bloom & branches bud
across the fields & through the wood.
The lily's luminescent glow
beams out & greets me, as you know,   440

[23]

her countenance – so bright & fair –
inviting me to fly to her.
The rose as well, her face of fire
emerging from a thorny briar,
imploring me to stir & sing 445
her praises with some loving hymn.
I sing both night & day, therefore,
& if it pleases I sing more,
enchanting people with my song
though careful not to sing too long, 450
for when I witness happy men
I know to stop indulging them;
once my performance is complete
I choose to make a wise retreat.
When men attend their ripened sheaves 455
& greenness withers from the leaves,
that's when I turn & take my leave,
migrating far from winter's reach;
I see the weather turning &
I head off to my native land, 460
but not before I'm thanked & loved
for toiling in this neighbourhood.
Yes, once the task is carried out
I'm gone! Why would I hang about?
It's neither prudent nor inspired 465
to linger longer than required.'

he Owl considered what she'd heard,
    digested each & every word
    & pondered how she might redress
such comments in her next address,   470
for those aware of verbal tricks
must cautiously assess the risks.

he Owl replied, 'You ask me why
    all winter through I call & cry.
    Well, it's a common trait of man   475
& has been since the world began
    that worthy friends will congregate
    with worthy friends to celebrate;
at table, in the home, good folk
exchanging mirth & pleasant talk,   480
particularly at Christmas time
when rich & poor & low & high
will sing their carols night & day.
I like to help them when I may,
but my concerns & cares belong   485
to deeper things than games & song,
to wit, I have a smart response
which I'll communicate at once.
In summer, heady feelings reign
that meddle with a fellow's brain   490
& turn his pure, unsullied mind

to notions of a lustful kind,
& not one living thing can wait
to mount his mate & copulate,
& frisky stallions in the stud   495
would ride each filly if they could.
And you're the centre of the throng
with your debauched, licentious song.
So when it's time to do the deed
you brag about your need to breed,   500
but once your wanton act is done
you're spent, & suddenly struck dumb,
or cackle with a blue tit's voice
& make a cracked & croaky noise.
In fact your song's worse than a sparrow's,   505
grubbing through the stubbled furrows;
once desire has run its course
your throat dries up & leaves you hoarse.
Throughout the summer months the yokels
writhe & wriggle, but those locals   510
aren't possessed by love – their limbs & loins
are at the mercy of their groins.
And when his primal urge has passed
a man's great ardour will collapse;
he worms his way inside a skirt   515
then falls down lifeless & inert.
It's very similar with your mood:
the day you nestle on your brood
your song comes to a sudden stop
& on your perch your bolt is shot;   520
once all the thrills & spills are done

it leaves you with a slackened tongue.
But when the nights turn long & dark
& bitter frost lies deep & sharp
then soon enough it's obvious   525
who's resolute & vigorous.
It's during hardship that we find
who goes ahead, who lags behind,
& who among us doesn't shirk
when delegated to the work.   530
That's when I'm at my liveliest
& singing at my blissful best.
In winter months I'm never vexed
because I'm not some feeble wretch.
I comfort creatures that are known   535
to have no courage of their own,
the apprehensive & forlorn
who long for somewhere safe & warm.
I often sing them my refrain
as consolation for their pain.   540
At which point shall I rest my case?
Are you out-thought? Put in your place?'

The Nightingale said, 'No. Now listen
closely to my next submission.
There's no verdict on this bout   545
as yet. Be calm & hear me out,
I'll win it with a single move
which no appealing will disprove.'

That isn't fair,' the Owl complained.
'As promised you have made your claims   550
which I have answered, as you know.
Before we seek a judgement, though,
I mean to score a point or two
& speak as I've been spoken to,
so if you're able do reply.   555
You sorry creature, please describe
what other purpose you fulfil
apart from being very shrill!
Your only talent as a critter
seems to be your endless witter,   560
& you're puny & you sport
a mantle that's unseemly short.
You're no more use to other men
than the pathetic little wren,
& what advancement ever came   565

from those whose singing sounds insane?
Plus, once your song has petered out
you've nothing else to brag about.
Wise Alfred said – & well he might
since it is absolutely right –   570
that none are loved for very long
just for their aptitude for song,
& it's a useless, worthless thing
that can't do any more than sing.
You're empty but for chirping chatter,   575
nothing else about you matters.
And you're dirty, drab, & look
no better than a ball of soot.
You lack all prettiness & strength
& come up short in height & length.   580
If Beauty called it didn't stay,
& Virtue looked the other way.
Another charge that I will file:
your habits, like your looks, are vile.
Arriving at a person's plot   585
where thorns & branches knit & knot
by hedgerows & by tangled weeds
where people go to squat & pee,
that's where you like to hang around
& won't withdraw to cleaner ground.   590
At night, while I pursue the mouse
you loiter by that smelly house
perched on a nettle or a reed,
at song behind the toilet seat.

It's there you frequently appear,   595
where people bend & bare their rear.
Disdainfully you say I eat
all kinds of squalid insect meat,
yet hypocritically you lunch
on horrid flies & spiders, munch   600
through worms & creepy-crawly bugs
found in the tree bark where you grub.
I undertake essential tasks
where people live, performing acts
that folk find helpful, doing good   605
where humans house their stock of food.
I prey on vermin dusk to dawn
both in the church & in the barn.
It is my pleasure in Christ's house
to hunt down every filthy mouse;   610
no rodent will live safely there
while I patrol it from the air.
Alternatively I might choose
some different dwelling for my roost:
great trees stand in the wood, & there   615
the sturdy boughs are never bare
but overgrown with ivy vines
whose leafy tendrils intertwine,
whose verdant tones are never lost
through any weather, snow or frost.   620
My stronghold in those trunks & arms –
in summer cool, in winter warm –
is always green & always bright
when yours has disappeared from sight.

[30]

Another groundless charge you lay   625
insults my little chicks. You say
their nest is sullied by their faeces –
this is true of many species:
stabled horses, oxen in their stalls,
all leave their droppings where they fall,   630
& infant children in their cots,
of lowly birth, of courtly stock,
do certain things when newly born
they cease to do when fully grown.
To blame the fledgling is unjust;   635
it toilets when & where it must.
An ancient proverb wisely states:
"The crone will sprint if need dictates."
A further issue: I suggest
you come with me & see my nest.   640
By noting how it's organised
you'll be enlightened – if you're wise.
Within a wide & hollow space
my fledglings have their bedding place,
but interlocked around the edge   645
the criss-crossed lattice forms a ledge
& there my youngsters void their bowels.
What practice you suggest, we owls
forbid. We watch man build his home
then in its image build our own.   650
All human beings build their loos
close to their homes & we do too.
They value such convenience –
we want the same experience!

Now stop your chelping, chatterbox,   655
you've never been so tied in knots.
To my remarks you've no riposte;
hang up your axe, your case is lost.'

Those comments stunned the Nightingale;
she tried to answer back, but failed.   660
She racked her brains, at pains to find
a clear example in her mind
that proved her usefulness, one thing
that she could do apart from sing,
& had to squash the other's claim   665
or lose advantage in the game,
though it's not easy to rebut
contentions that are so well put.
The man whose self-assurance slips
must turn to scheming & to wit   670
& use the language of disguise.
When talking he should improvise
so that his mouth does not reveal
the feelings that his mind conceals,
& arguments will fall apart   675
when out of kilter with the heart
& words depart from their design
when heart & tongue are misaligned.

Any yet, by means well known to some,
such obstacles are overcome: 680
the brain is at its cunning best
when challenged by a crucial test,
& when a prize is most at risk
the mind devises crafty tricks.
As Alfred's ancient proverb tells   685
(an adage we remember well):
'Not till the worst predicament
is resolution imminent.'
For guile not only comes alive
at crisis point, it truly thrives,   690
so no man is a helpless cause
while artfulness directs his course,
but if his bag of tricks should split
inventive thoughts slip through the slit,
& once resourcefulness departs   695
all schemes & tactics fall apart.
As Alfred said both well & true
(& Alfred knew a thing or two):
'When out & out disaster looms
a remedy will follow soon.'   700

herefore the Nightingale, though pressed,
stood poised to do her very best,
because the stresses & the strains
had urged the bird to rack her brains
& stage the kind of argument 705
required by her predicament.

The Nightingale said, 'Owl, you ask
why I pursue no other task
than singing out my summer airs
& spreading pleasure everywhere. 710
And yet my single art transcends
the whole of your accomplishments:
one song of mine has greater worth
than all the Owl songs on this earth.
Now listen to me & you'll learn 715
why man was born: it was to yearn
for all the bliss in heaven's domain
where joyful singing never wanes,
towards which those of virtue strive
as best they can throughout their lives. 720
That's why there's singing in the kirks
& holy clerks perform their works,
so man will know by means of song
where he is bound & will belong,
& rather than forget the bliss 725

will ponder it & make it his,
& understand from hearing hymns
what great rejoicing heaven brings.
All canons, monks & clerks, at home
in good communities, are known   730
to rise from sleep when midnight strikes
& sing in praise of heaven's light,
& priests from country parishes
will sing as night-time vanishes,
& I assist as best I can   735
by singing day & night to man,
&, heartened by my trilling, he
sings out himself more willingly.
All prudent people, I announce,
should keep a cheerful countenance,   740
& strive to hear their whole life long
the sound of that eternal song.
And so, Owl, you can sit & rot,
because such feuding fails, & what
we cannot settle on our own   745
should go before the Pope in Rome.
However, wait a while, for there
are other matters to be aired,
& telling words you won't escape
if England's future were at stake!   750
Why do you say I'm understrength
& small in size & short in length,
& why insist that I'm not strong
because I'm neither tall nor long?
You are deluded in your aims   755

[37]

to smear me with deceitful claims,
for I'm ingenious & shrewd
& not a little self-assured,
well versed in song & many sorts
of tricks – I don't rely on force.   760
Because it's true what Alfred said:
"The fist is conquered by the head."
A streak of canniness prevails
where means of might & muscle fail,
& towns & citadels will fall   765
with very little force at all,
since guile makes walls come crashing down,
throws knights on horseback to the ground.
Raw strength is worthless, but the brain
will triumph time & time again;   770
look where you please, it's evident
good sense has no equivalent.
A man is weaker than a horse
but lacking nous a horse is forced
to bear great burdens on its back   775
& feel the strain of plough & tack,
withstand the spur & whip, endure
being tethered by the millhouse door,
& through its ignorance must do
exactly what man tells it to,   780
&, strong as it might be, obey
what even tiny children say.
Though man has strength, it is his mind
leaves other creatures far behind;
collective vigour never can   785

stand equal to the wit of man,
& so through intellect man shall
rule over every animal.
I manage more with just one song
than you achieve the whole year long.   790
For my great talent I am loved,
for being brutish you are snubbed.
And so I ask, do you think ill
of me because I have one skill?
A pair of wrestlers in a fight   795
will huff & puff with all their might.
The first knows many different throws
& tactics to deceive his foe,
the second only has one move
but as a ploy it always proves   800
victorious; with speed he scores
by dropping rivals to the floor,
& since it works why would that man
be forced to find a different plan?
You say you offer many types   805
of service – we are not alike –
& all your attributes combined
don't match this special skill of mine.
While hounds pursue a fox, a cat
knows how to sidestep the attack   810
although he only has one ruse.
The fox has many tricks to use
& thinks he'll give the dogs the slip,
but his deceits aren't up to it.
He knows paths straight & crooked, how   815

to dangle from a branch or bough
until the hound gives up the trail
& – heading for the moor – turns tail.
The fox can creep along the hedge
& knows how best to slink & edge   820
down different tracks, then double back
to bring confusion, till the pack
has lost its bearings & is sent
in all directions from the scent.
His twists & turns being done, that's when   825
the fox heads for his earthen den,
& yet for all his crafty ways
his clever scheming never pays;
he's fast & fleet, but he'll be caught
& ripped out of his red fur coat.   830
The cat's one skill will never fail:
both on the hill & in the vale
he climbs up trees with such aplomb
his grey pelt stays where it belongs!
All this holds true about myself,   835
my single skill defeats your twelve.'

'Hold on, hold on,' exclaimed the Owl,
'your arguments are false & foul.
You offer such a clever spoof
it sounds as if you speak the truth, 840
& deal in verbal trickery
so plausible & slippery
that every individual
believes your every syllable!
But wait a while. *I'll* be believed 845
when I describe how you deceive
& fabricate, & I'll expose
your way of speaking as a hoax.
You boast you lead the human race
with song towards some higher place 850
where singing happens ceaselessly,
& this is what displeases me,
this flabbergasting fib, this boast
of acting as some special host
to God's estate with just a tune. 855
No, no, they'll find out soon
how much they have to pray & cry
to seek redemption from their crimes
before they get to enter there,
& I advise them to prepare, 860
insisting they must weep, not sing,
before their journey can begin.
Before they leave their earthly home
all men, as sinners, should atone
through crying, till the tears they weep 865
make bitter what they thought was sweet.

[43]

God knows I sing because I'm fair
& not to catch men in a snare.
My song of longing carries tones
of lamentations in its notes, 870
so man will know his crimes & grieve
his misdemeanours; he'll believe
the song I'm singing, urging him
to own his guilt & mourn his sins.
Disputing it won't change a thing, 875
I blubber better than you sing,
& right will triumph over wrong –
my weeping's better than your song.

And while some citizens are kind,
good in their hearts & pure of mind, 880
they pine to leave this earthly sphere,
regretting their existence here;
as people they are saved, & yet
they see a world of woe, & shed
their salty tears for other men 885
& pray Christ's mercy reaches them.
I help both good & bad because
my mouth brings balm to either cause.
I aid the good when longing burns
by singing to them while they yearn, 890
& sing to sinning men as well
to show them all where sorrows dwell.
I counter you, & will besmirch
your claims. While singing from your perch
you conjure sordid visions in 895
the minds of those men listening,

& lose your right to heaven's bliss
because your tune is heaven-less,
& lacking holiness you sing
of lewdness & no other thing.   900
No one mistakes your whistled cry
for priestly chants in church. And I
have yet another charge to lay –
let's see you argue this away.
Why don't you sing on foreign ground   905
where there's a need for such a sound?
In Ireland's realms you never call
nor visit Scotland's lands at all,
nor Norway's, & don't serenade
the populace of Galloway.   910
Of any song beneath the sun
what knowledge have those people? None.
Why won't you use your songs to reach
those unenlightened priests, & teach
the clergy with your singing voice   915
how angels in the heavens rejoice?
You're like a useless spring that teems
close by a swiftly rushing stream
but leaves the hill-slopes dehydrated,
flowing off, entirely wasted.   920
North & south I travel &
they know of me in every land.
Both near & distant, east & west
I do again what I do best
which is to cry out in alarm   925
about your song's deluding charm.

I caution people, when I sing,
to guard against excessive sin;
in fact I urge them all to stop
before they tie themselves in knots.   930
I preach that now's the time to weep,
not next time, in the devil's keep!'

T he Nightingale was now inflamed,
    & not a little bit ashamed,
    because the Owl had dared to scorn   935
the perching site where she performed:
behind the loo, among the weeds,
where people crap & people pee.
She mulled things over for a while,
being well aware of how, when riled,   940
a man is prone to lose his mind.
For as King Alfred once opined:
'The voice of hate is doomed to fail,
& anger pleads to no avail.'
Because when rage stirs up the blood   945
it surges in a frenzied flood,
& overwhelms the heart until
all reason clouds, all senses fill
with darkness, & without a light
the mind is blind to truth & right.   950
Accordingly the Nightingale

kept calm, & did not shout or wail;
she'd make a stronger argument
if she controlled her temperament.

'Now listen to me, Owl,' she said,   955
'since it's a slippy slope you tread.
    You say we skulk behind the house:
    it's true, that territory's ours,
    for where a lord & lady lie
    we perch & sing our songs close by.   960
Do you believe the wise man should
avoid the true road due to mud?
Or that tomorrow's sun won't shine
because you nest in layers of grime?
Why would a hole cut in a seat   965
encourage me to seek retreat
from singing in the very place
where lord & ladyship embrace?
It is my duty & my right
to live at such a lofty height.   970
And yet you boast about your song,
claim it's so striking & so strong
it urges humans to repent
by ululating their lament.
Should people holler their distress   975
as if resigned to hopelessness?

Because if every person screeched
like you they'd terrify the priest.
Man should be calm & bite his tongue
& quietly confess his wrongs, 980
& only when the Lord is praised
should songs be sung & voices raised;
in church, at fitting hours, no song
can ever be too loud or long.
Your voice is filled with tears & gloom, 985
I sing a joyous & delightful tune.
You might well carry on & cry
relentlessly, until you die,
continuing to bawl & shout
till both your eyes come bursting out. 990
Which man is best, do you believe,
the glad man or the man of grief?
Our lives could be described like this:
your life of glumness, mine of bliss.
You also fail to understand 995
why I don't sing in foreign lands.
No thanks! What joy could I provoke
in such morose & gloomy folk?
Those ugly realms are formed of tracts
of wilderness, where rocks & crags 1000
reach skywards, & whose people know
of little more than hail & snow.
Such horrible & wretched lands
breed savage, melancholy clans,
who have no harmony or peace 1005
in their disordered tribes, & feast

[48]

on bloody fish & meat that looks
like wolf-torn flesh, & from their cups
they glug down both the whey & milk.
They lack enlightenment, that ilk   1010
who brew no beer or wine, whose lives
are feral & uncivilised,
who go about in shaggy pelts
as if they'd wandered out of hell.
The good man, heading for their home   1015
(as one did recently, from Rome)
to teach the sinful & depraved
how decent, upright folk behave
might just as well stay put, because
he'll waste time on a fruitless cause.   1020
Far easier to teach a bear
to hold a shield & hurl a spear
than kindle in that motley throng
the least desire to hear my song.
My efforts there won't change a thing;   1025
however many hours I sing
those savages will never alter,
not if bridle nor if halter
brought their habits to an end
or steel & iron threatened them.   1030
And yet in pleasant, calmer climes
where natives think with saner minds
I exercise my vocal cords.
Such worthy work brings great reward
to those who listen to my hymns;   1035
the church's songs are what I sing.

[49]

The ancient statutes used to say
(with wisdom that holds true today)
that man should only plant a field
on soil that brings a healthy yield;   1040
it's lunacy to plough & sow
where crops & flowers will not grow.'

The angry Owl was so provoked
her eyes grew wider as she spoke.
'You claim to guard the bower where   1045
the leaves grow & the flowers flare
& couples sleep, that sheltered place
where lovers lie down & embrace.
But once you sang – I know for sure –
outside a marriage suite, to lure   1050
a lady into wicked ways.
To lead her body to disgrace
you sang tunes of a shameful sort
& filled her dreams with carnal thoughts.
His lordship soon became aware;   1055
with lime & every type of snare
he laid his traps to make a catch,
&, landing at the window's hatch,
you came to justice, being pinned
& fastened firmly by your shins.   1060
The punishment your crime would bring:

wild horses tore you limb from limb.
So do your worst with maids & wives
by bringing ruin to their lives;
your tongue will prove the very trap   1065
that leaves you floored & in a flap.'

The Nightingale, piqued at these words,
    would readily have fought with swords
      & spears if she had been a man,
but since she had no choice her plan   1070
involved her sharp & clever tongue.
    'Who speaks well . . . fights well,' goes the song;
she'd wage war with her voice instead.
'To fight well, speak well,' Alfred said.

Your talk won't cover me in shame –   1075
    his lordship was the one to blame
      for being jealous of his wife.
His envy could have cost his life
because his heart began to fail
when she conversed with other males.   1080
He locked her in an inner chamber;

[51]

strong & steadfast bounds contained her;
sorry for her anguish there
I felt her pain & pitied her
& kept her cheerful all day long   1085
by filling every hour with song,
a tactic which enraged the knight
who loathed my bones with all his might.
He tried to make his problem mine
but was found guilty of the crime: 1090
on hearing of that man's misdeed

 King Henry, rest in peace, decreed
the sentence must be banishment,
a right & proper punishment
for acts so base & underhand   1095
committed in a good king's land,
whereby a tiny Nightingale
had been dismembered top to tail.
To bring back honour to my race
he wiped the smile from that man's face   1100
& made him pay one hundred pounds
to me. My chicks, now safe & sound,
enjoy their new prosperity
by right, & their security.
And I, avenged of the offence,   1105
speak with a strengthened confidence.
Because of that one incident
my cheerfulness is permanent
& as I please I raise my voice
& no one dares dispute my choice.   1110
But you, you wretch, you ghoulish ghost,

you can't identify a post
or hollow stump to crouch inside
avoiding those who'd nip your hide.
For youngsters, serfs & those who farm,   1115
& peasant folk, all mean you harm,
& if they spy you on your perch
they hope to injure you, or worse,
& fill their pockets up with stones
then aim to break your horrid bones.   1120
It's only when you're struck or shot
that people find your body's got
some kind of use: your loathsome neck
& trunk, hung on a stick, deflect
all kinds of hungry birds & beasts   1125
who eye man's corn crops as their feast.
There's no worth in your flesh & blood
though as a scarecrow you're quite good
wherever seeds are newly sown,
for sparrow, goldfinch, rook & crow   1130
will never venture near the clod
where your corpse dangles from a rod.
Each springtime, when the blossom's out
& young seeds germinate then sprout,
no famished bird would ever dare   1135
go near them if you're swinging there.
You're vile & foul when drawing breath
& only valuable in death.
So now it's irrefutable
that you are far from beautiful   1140
when you're alive, because those birds,

who shrieked when your grim form disturbed
their eyes, are still spooked by your looks
when you're deceased & on a hook.
You're viewed with scorn, & rightly so,   1145
for always singing songs of woe,
reminding folk of things they hate
from early morning until late.
Your terrifying call gives fright
to those who hear it in the night.   1150
Your cry's a sign of certain doom:
it says a man will perish soon
or lose his property, or spells
the ruin of a friend, foretells
a house-fire, or of being mobbed   1155
by violent thugs, or being robbed,
or hints at plague among the herd,
or human sickness, or brings word
that widowhood awaits the wife,
or points to conflict & to strife.   1160
You sing of human strain & stress –
all those who hear you feel depressed –
& never sing at all unless
you're trumpeting some great distress.
And therefore you are vilified;   1165
you're thrashed & pelted, folks let fly
with sticks & stones & sods & peat
until there's nowhere to retreat.
You're like a cursed town crier who's
forever spouting sorry news,   1170
a herald with an evil cry

whose proclamations terrify.
May you be subject to the wrath
of all those wearing linen cloth.'

The Owl did not delay for long,   1175
her answer came back loud & strong.
'Have you become ordained? You preach
without the backing of the priest,
& act as though you *are* a priest,
which you are not, not in the least!   1180
I never heard you sing the Mass
& yet you curse at will, & pass
snide comments, blackening my name
through malice, time & time again.
To which there is a swift reply: 1185
"Move over," is the carter's cry.
Why does my power, wit & vision
draw from you such crude derision?
I am wise & no mistake,
& know which paths the future takes.   1190
I forecast famine, war, the age
a person will achieve, & gauge
when wives will lose their husbands, &
when vengeful strife will haunt the land.
I know who'll dangle from a noose,   1195
who'll meet a grisly end, who'll lose

their life in combat – hear the call
of warfare, fight their battle, fall.
Which cows will suffer from disease,
which beasts will soon be on their knees,   1200
if trees will bloom, if corn will grow –
all of these things I know. I know
which houses will be burnt to soot,
who'll go by carriage, who on foot,
which ships will sink in heavy seas,   1205
which smiths will rivet faulty seams.
I know all this & more besides;
through reading books I'm very wise,
& from the gospels have worked out
more than I care to talk about.   1210
I often go to church & find
the lessons there improve my mind,
therefore the power to divine
is one of many skills of mine;
I know before the hue & cry   1215
who's being hunted down, & why.
And yet my talent leaves me cross
& sad while sitting here, because
I see misfortune is about
to find its prey, & I cry out;   1220
I warn folk to be vigilant
& plan for future incidents.
A clever lesson Alfred taught
that should remain within our thoughts:
"A threat seen in its infancy   1225
will lose much of its potency."

[58]

So heavy jolts have far less force
if spotted early in their course;
& you can dodge an arrow's blow
by watching as it leaves the bow,   1230
then keeping its approach in sight,
then ducking from its fatal flight.
And when a man encounters shame
or harm, why must I take the blame?
I know what trouble to expect   1235
but I am not its architect.
So, if a blind man lost his way,
& you observed that fellow stray
from his intended path, & pitch
into a stinking, muddy ditch,   1240
don't claim the sorry consequence
was brought on by my prescience.
My mind detects things in advance,
so when I'm sitting on my branch
I know with perfect clarity   1245
when mishap or calamity
will strike a man, but don't blame me
for seeing things that he can't see.
Should I be made to bear the blame
because I have the better brain?   1250
When I see misery or harm
approach I cry out in alarm,
& beg that people be on guard
before disaster hits them hard.
But if my call is soft or shrill   1255
whatever happens is God's will.

So why do people grumble when
the truth I utter troubles them?
I can't bring misadventure near
by warning of it for a year,   1260
I sing so folk will understand
catastrophe is close at hand.
Yes, when I hoot some dark event
is heralded as imminent.
For nobody remains secure   1265
forever; we can be assured
that danger, even when concealed,
is no less threatening or real.
King Alfred coined this fitting truth
(& his word was the gospel truth):   1270
"The better-off the man," he said,
"the more that man must plan ahead."
Despite what riches might be his
a man can't trust to wealth. There is
no heat that can't go off the boil,   1275
no purest white that can't be soiled,
no love that can't resort to hate,
no joy that can't infuriate.
Like earthly bliss all things must pass.
Eternity alone will last.   1280
Presumably you'll now accept
your arguments lack intellect,
since all the slurs & slights you spread
return & sully you instead.
What's more, you suffer at the hand   1285
of every punch you try to land.

Whatever your malign intent
each jibe becomes a compliment,
so start afresh, rethink your claim
or shame's the only prize you'll gain.'   1290

he Nightingale was flummoxed now.
She sat & sighed, disarmed by how
the Owl had verbalised her case
& put her in an awkward place
with words that left her lost & vexed   1295
& worried what to argue next.
But she was smart, & in exchange
replied: 'What? Owl, are you deranged?
You state that you can prophesise,
but how did you become so wise?   1300
Perhaps your teacher was a witch,
a charge you'll have to answer, wretch,
to stay among the human race,
or else you'll have to flee this place.
For those who deal in mystic arts   1305
are scorned by priests & must depart
the Faith; & since you still insist
on witchery, your ban persists.
I made this clear not long ago,
then brazenly you asked to know   1310
if I'd become a priest or not,

but people curse you such a lot
that even living in a land
devoid of priests you'd still be damned,
for children speak of you as "foul",   1315
& adults as "the worthless Owl".
I've heard that prophecy relies
on readings of the starry skies
to make predictions that come true,
as you have often claimed to do.   1320

But you know nothing of the stars,
you only watch them from afar
like any man or animal
who boasts no special oracle.
An ape can take a long hard look   1325
at every page inside a book
then close it, & know nothing more
of any theory or law.
And you are no anomaly,
a stranger to astrology.   1330
Yet you persist with your assault,
you rogue, & say that I'm at fault
for singing close to fellows' houses,
meaning to corrupt their spouses.
But you speak dishonestly;   1335
no marriage failed because of me,
though I admit I call & sing
to girls & women, & the thing
I sing about is love, it's true.
I want good women to pursue   1340
the love between a married pair

& not resort to an affair;
I urge young maidens not to chase
the kind of love that brings disgrace
but satisfy their hearts as wives   1345
who love their husbands all their lives.
This is the message I promote,
the essence of my every note.
A woman might not have enough
resolve (being made of finer stuff)   1350
to snub a suitor's compliments
or breathless sighs; if she relents
& misbehaves with him, don't claim
the fault is mine, that I'm to blame.
If love proves women pliable   1355
in no way am I liable;
if women plan to go astray
I'll go on singing anyway;
a woman can have fun in bed
for reasons either good or bad,   1360
& she'll interpret what I sing
as either virtue or as sin.
For there is nothing on this earth,
however notable its worth,
that can't be sullied or misused,   1365
as gold & silver are abused
when precious metals are exchanged
for vice or mischief. This explains
why weapons – good for keeping peace –
when owned illicitly by thieves   1370
are murderous weapons in their hands,

as is the case in foreign lands.
And it's no different with my voice:
sweet as it is, it can, by choice,
be twisted from the virtuous   1375
& used for wicked purposes.
But don't blame love – that's horrible.
For love is proud & honourable
between a man & woman, though
not stolen love; that love is low,   1380
the sordid, grubby type. Well may
the Holy Cross bring down its rage
on those who act unnaturally –
they must be mad. And actually
a woman is insane indeed   1385
who goes outside the nest to breed.
A female's flesh is very frail,
no wonder she's condemned to fail
if crude desire maintains its grip,
forever causing her to slip,   1390
though they are not completely lost
who stumble on the rocks of lust;
those overtaken by desire
have often risen from the mire.
And when it comes to sin & shame   1395
there are two different types to name:
the first is the licentious kind,
the second is a cast of mind.
The flesh leads men to drunken days
& lechery & idle ways;   1400
a troubled spirit leads to spite

[64]

& envy, & invokes delight
at men's misfortunes, fosters greed
& scoffs at kind & caring deeds,
belittles & derides the meek   1405
& swells with pompous pride. So speak
the truth: by rank, is flesh the first
of evils, or is spirit worse?
Admit, then, if you think it's true,
that flesh is least bad of the two,   1410
since many men, their souls enmeshed
with Satan's cause, are pure of flesh.
No person should go slandering
a woman's lowly hankerings,
& he who argues from that side   1415
commits the greater sin of pride.
Both wives & maidens, through my voice,
give in to passion, but my choice
would be the virgin every time –
your thoughts will no doubt echo mine   1420
once you have heard my argument
from its beginning to its end.
A virgin, by her nature, may
succumb to lust & lose her way
but still be lifted up & saved   1425
no matter how she misbehaves,
because by taking marriage vows
she'll rid herself of guilt; her spouse
was once her lover, but the pair
are now excused of their affair.   1430
The man she trysted with at night

is hers now every day, by right.
A young girl doesn't understand
& so obeys her heart's commands;
the reckless fellow leads her on   1435
with every tactic known to man:
he comes & goes, insists & begs,
harangues her then plays hard to get,
implores her, pleads with her so long,
can she be blamed if things go wrong?   1440
She didn't know the dangers, so
she thought she'd give the thing a go,
experimenting with the game
that makes the wild & frisky tame.
Through pity, then, I can't resist   1445
delivering a song of bliss
when witnessing the painful trace
that love leaves in a young girl's face.
I try to teach them, through my song,
love of that kind will not last long,   1450
because, just as my song relents,
love rarely stays when it descends
on children's hearts, but meets its death
the way that warmth fades on our breath.
I sing my song to them, its flow   1455
beginning high & ending low,
until the melody subsides
& shortly afterwards it dies;
on hearing that my song has passed
girls understand that love won't last,   1460
because my song's a gasp of air

that briefly lives then disappears.
Through me, young women turn
away from ignorance & learn
that dizzy passion, like my tune,   1465
will fade away, & all too soon.
Believe me, though, I'm horrified
when married women cheat & lie.
A wife should note: I sing no song
while I am pregnant with my young.   1470
A marriage might be firmly forged
but flirty fools should be ignored;
I am both sickened & amazed
that men, at times, are so depraved
they have the nerve to go to bed   1475
with someone else's wife instead.
Two explanations I have heard
& will relate, but not a third:
the husband here is either brave
or he's a weak & worthless knave.   1480
If he's a bold & manly sort
nobody with a brain would court
his wife until she parts her legs;
that fool would end up hurt or dead
or lose what dangles from his groin   1485
& never feel desire again!
And even if he's not afraid
it's still a dirty, low-down trade,
offending decent gentlemen
by sleeping with their wives. And then   1490
we have the other sort, inept

[69]

with food & worse in bed; expect
no love when men so grossly fat
roll on their wives & squash them flat,
when oafs like that reach for their wives 1495
to grope & fumble at their thighs.
So, of those two adulteries
the first results in injury,
the second in embarrassment;
through acts of brutal harassment 1500
the husband who is tough will harm
the man who takes his woman's arm,
but if her man's a wretch it must
reduce the lover to disgust,
imagining the worthless dregs 1505
who've writhed between the woman's legs.
No man with any self-respect
could sleep with her, should he reflect
what types she's entertained before;
no love would last there any more.' 1510

The Owl was glad to hear this tale,
because although the Nightingale
had started speaking well enough
her argument had tapered off.
She said, 'From what you have described   1515
it's clear your sympathies reside
with girls; they're faultless in your eyes,
therefore you praise them to the skies.
But married women, filled with grief,
all turn to me to seek relief.   1520
It happens time & time again
that married life comes under strain,
because of which the husband strays
& finds some other love to chase,
immorally pursuing her   1525
& tipping out his purse on her,
abandoning his lawful spouse
who occupies their lonely house
in threadbare clothes, among bare walls,
with very little food at all.   1530
And out of terror she has learned
to bite her lip once he's returned,
though like a lunatic he shouts
& bawls & throws his weight about.
All that she does displeases him,   1535
all that she utters teases him,
& when she tries to keep the peace
he's apt to punch her in the teeth.
The man who misbehaves that way
can't fail to send his wife astray.   1540

[71]

Because of his abuse at home
she'll seek out pleasures of her own;
she'll cuckold him, of course she will,
but don't say she's responsible.
And yes, it's usually the case   1545
she's well brought up & fair of face,
so when the husband spends his purse
outside the home the crime seems worse –
the mistress of his love affair
is barely worth one strand of hair   1550
belonging to his spouse. In life
such husbands fail to trust their wives:
no other men must talk to them,
& if they look at other men
or speak with other men politely   1555
husbands think deceit is likely.
Stifled, then, by lock & key,
the wives turn to adultery,
because they're driven to explore
what was anathema before.   1560
A curse on those who whine & whinge
when wives deliver their revenge.
This is the thing that wives complain
to me about; I feel their pain
& sense such overwhelming hurt   1565
I sometimes think my heart will burst.
My eyes are sore with bitter tears;
I pray that Christ our Lord will hear
their prayers so wives might share their beds
with decent, honest men instead.   1570

And now I'll tell you one thing more
that you will have no answer for,
I'll put your logic in a spin
& no reply will save your skin.
So, many merchants, many knights,   1575
will love their wives & treat them right,
& many peasants will do too;
accordingly each wife stays true,
& does her best to serve her lord
both in the bedroom & at board   1580
& eagerly she'll aim to please
with caring words & thoughtful deeds.
The husband travels far & wide
in his endeavours to provide
for them, & when he ups & leaves   1585
the steadfast wife at home will grieve;
she'll sit & sigh when he departs
because a longing fills her heart
&, anxious for her husband's sake,
she'll fret by day then lie awake;   1590
each moment lasts a long, long while,
& every step feels like a mile.

Outside, alone, at night, I keep
a vigil while the world's asleep;
alert to how bereft she is   1595
I sing songs for her benefit,
laments for her unhappiness

expressing just how sad she is,
& for this show of sympathy
she warms to me & welcomes me.   1600

I strive to help such wives because
they seek to plot a noble course.
You've riled my heart to such a stage
it's almost paralysed with rage
& I can barely speak a word,   1605
but I'll continue, undeterred.
You say that I'm despised by men,
inspire hostility in them;
they threaten me with stones & sticks
then beat & smash my bones to bits   1610
& when all life in me is lost
they hang me from a hedge or post
to scare the magpie & the crow
in acres where the crops are sown.
And so, in truth, by shedding blood   1615
I'm helping out & doing good!
My death brings people benefit
which you find painful to admit,
for once you're shrivelled up & gone
you are no use to anyone.   1620
Why you exist I just don't know
you good-for-nothing so-&-so,
but even when I cease to live
I still have something more to give:
when hunters mount me on a stick   1625
in woods where trees grow dense & thick
I serve my purpose as a lure
for little birds, so I ensure
men have their share of roasted meat
by snaring food they like to eat.   1630

[74]

You're just as pointless when alert
as when you're lifeless & inert;
why bother bringing up a brood –
alive or dead they do no good.'

The Nightingale took in this stance   1635
    then hopped up to a higher branch
    & settled on a blossomed bough.
'Look, Owl,' she said, 'be careful now,
I won't react to you again
    because all sense has left your brain.   1640
You boast that you infuriate,
that you're the object of man's hate,
& with that wailing, hooting blare
you wallow in your own despair.
You say that lads set up their snares   1645
then let you dangle in the air
& tear you limb from limb, or make
a scarecrow from you, on a stake.
It seems to me you've lost the game
by trumpeting your acts of shame;   1650
it seems that you concede the case
by glorifying your disgrace.'
Once she had said her piece she searched
& found a lovely place to perch
then tuned the workings of her throat   1655

[77]

to find the most resounding notes
& sang so piercingly & clear
that birds flocked in from far & near,
the oriole & mistle thrush
& song thrush – big birds, small birds – rushed   1660
towards the scene on hearing that
the Nightingale had won the spat
& from the branches they gave voice
as if the trees themselves rejoiced,
& jeered the Owl, as if her vice   1665
were gambling, & she'd lost at dice!

On hearing this the Owl replied:
    'You've called an army to your side?
        But do you really want to fight,
    you stunted little featherweight?   1670
    What are your allies shouting for?
    If you propose to wage a war
you'll learn before you next take flight
what strength my family has, what might,
for all those enemies of yours   1675
with curving beaks & pointed claws
are kin of mine, & if I send
for their assistance they'll attend,
among their ranks the fighting cock,
who would be right to cast his lot   1680

with me – we both have striking cries
& both sit under starry skies.
Were I to raise the battle cry
I'd rally so much infantry
your pride would fall to pieces, bird.   1685
You & your kind aren't worth a turd,
& by the time the sun has set
you'll all be featherless. We met
with an agreement in this place
that fairness would decide our case,   1690
with honest rules to be observed
by which true justice would be served.
Now I suspect you'll break that pact;
you fear the verdict so you act
without fair judgement being reached,   1695
& want to brawl instead, you wretch.
So I advise you – change your mind
before I cross the battle line;
be smart & quickly fly away
& live to fight another day.   1700
For if my legions mobilise
then by these talons which I prize
you'll sing a very different song
& curse all wars from this day on,
because not one of you can stare   1705
me in the face – you wouldn't dare.'
The Owl was forceful in her speech;
of course she hadn't yet beseeched
her troops to fight her cause, but railed
this way against the Nightingale   1710

[79]

for men have stood on battlefields
quite powerless, despite their shields,
despite the sharpness of their spears,
yet filled their enemies with fear
& caused their foes to quake & sweat   1715
through warlike acts & hostile threats.

That morning, though, the wood had seen
the wren's arrival on the scene;
she'd come to help the Nightingale
because although her voice is small   1720
it rings out loud & sharp & clear
& brings enjoyment to the ear.
The wren's intelligence was praised;
that little bird had not been raised
in woods, but in the world of men,   1725
& her astuteness came from them.
So she could sing out anywhere
(including if the king was there).
She said, 'Now let me make my speech.
Do you intend to break the peace   1730
& put our royal king to shame
when he is neither dead nor lame?
You'll suffer harm & moral stain
by trading blows in his domain.
The two of you should call a truce   1735

then go in search of rightful truth
& let a judgement be decreed,
as was initially agreed.'

The Nightingale said, 'Count me in.
    Not out of deference to the wren   1740
    but through my reverence for the law.
    It wouldn't suit me if this score
    was settled by injustice; I'll
    be more than happy standing trial.
And yes, I promised to engage   1745
that clever Simon Armitage
to take the role of magistrate –
& still have hopes he'll arbitrate,
but where shall we report to him?'
The wren, perched on a lime tree limb,   1750
said, 'Don't you know?' And then revealed,
'He's domiciled near Huddersfield,
in Yorkshire, nowhere near the sea
& nowhere near an estuary.
That's where he lives, & in that town   1755
he thinks wise thoughts & writes them down;
as far as Scotland life is better,
all because he's good with letters.
Finding him won't cause much strife,
he lives a solitary life,   1760

a shame for anyone who's heard
the rumours of his crafted words
& stories of his clever deeds.
If bishops issued a decree
to share with him their revenues   1765
& rents, then Armitage could choose
to venture from his residence
& reach a wider audience.'

ndeed that's true.' the Owl exclaimed.
'Those wealthy men should be ashamed,   1770
not holding him in high regard,
not giving him his just reward,
a leading figure of his age.
And they are men who pay a wage
to family members, & who splash   1775
substantial sums on little brats.
Neglecting Armitage so long
confirms their guilt & proves them wrong.
But come, let's find the one who'll bring
conclusion to our quarrelling.'   1780

he Nightingale said, 'To his place
we'll go. But who'll present our case
& make submissions to him there?'

n that department have no fear,'
the Owl replied. 'All that was said   1785
I memorised from A to Z,
& if you think I deviate
then intervene & put me straight.'
    And with those words – without their troops
& followers – they took the route   1790
to Huddersfield, but what occurred
when claims & counterclaims were heard,
regrettably I can't relate –
here's where the poem terminates.

ACKNOWLEDGEMENTS

Several excerpts from this translation originally appeared on the BBC Radio 4 programme and podcast *The Poet Laureate Has Gone to His Shed.*

A facsimile edition of both original manuscripts of the poem, published by Oxford University Press for the Early English Text Society (1963), has been both a valuable companion and a totemic presence on my desk for the past three years or so. The definitive critical edition is Neil Cartlidge's *The Owl and the Nightingale* (Liverpool University Press, 2016; first published in 2001 by University of Exeter Press). That transcription and translation, including a comprehensive analysis, appendices, notes, bibliography and glossary, is indispensable to any student of the poem; I am indebted to its scholarship and grateful for its existence. Brian Stone's translation (Penguin Classics, 1988) also contains an invaluable commentary on the poem, especially in relation to its biblical and theological underpinnings. I have also drawn on transcriptions by Eric Gerald Stanley (Manchester University Press, 1981), J. W. H. Atkins (Cambridge University Press, 1922) and John Edwin Wells (D. C. Heath and Co., 1907). There are now innumerable internet resources dedicated to the transmission and translation of the poem, including Wessex Parallel Web Texts and the Corpus of Middle English Prose and Verse, often with dedicated glossaries or providing access to dictionaries of Middle English. I am grateful to all those academic institutions who have made their work on the poem available to visiting researchers, especially those granting public online access.